View from
30,000 Feet

D.K. Nash

PAGE PUBLISHING, INC.
Conneaut Lake, PA

First originally published by Page Publishing 2021

ISBN 978-1-6624-4100-4 (pbk)
ISBN 978-1-6624-4101-1 (digital)

Printed in the United States of America

Preface

In the beginning, pilots not only flew the airplane but also attended to passengers and their baggage; scared or sick passengers would have to fend for themselves.

In 1930, Ellen Church, a nurse herself, convinced an airline executive that a nurse would be an asset on the airplane and talked him into hiring her as the first airline hostess, thus creating a new profession for women in the workplace.

Later in 1933, the first stewardesses were registered nurses hired for the sole purpose of comforting and serving the passengers.

Being a nurse wasn't the only requirement for employment. They also had to be single, and weight and height were an important factor in the small fifteen-passenger Condor with its narrow aisles and low ceilings. For the stewardess, the weight limit was 118 pounds with a maximum height of five feet and four inches, and they had to be between twenty and twenty-six years old.

American Airways expressed the following service ethics on April 23, 1933—ten days before the first stewardess flight; it was to become their legacy.

> In general, it is the duty and responsibility of the stewardess aboard the plane to personally take care of the wants and comforts of our patrons, anticipating their wishes as much as possible, and to do this in such a way as to have our patrons remember this service long after the actual trip is completed. Courtesy costs nothing and pays big dividends. We want our patrons to talk about this service. We want first-time riders to become our regular patrons.

In those days, being a stewardess was a lot of hard work with long, tedious hours. Each flight, before the passengers boarded, the stewardess had to check seat belts, the cleanliness of the aircraft, and make sure catering, magazines, newspapers, and other needed supplies were on board the aircraft. While boarding, they assisted passengers and even helped put their luggage in the cargo compartments.

Inflight box lunches were served with coffee, tea, and milk (never alcoholic beverages). On long fifteen-hour flights such as coast-to-coast, hot food was served. Meals were cooked prior to the flight and kept warm in large insulated containers. Following the meal service, the stewardess transformed the forward part of the cabin into sleeping berths complete with bed linens and pillows (not an easy task on these low-altitude, turbulent flights), all while at the same time assisting with airsick passengers.

At the beginning of World War II, nurses were joining the Army Nurse Corps in great numbers to serve their country. Consequently, the growing shortage of nurses in civilian life and the increase in demand for stewardesses forced the airlines to drop the RN requirement to open it up for more applicants while still upholding the other requirements, including the single status, weight, height, and mandatory resignation at age thirty-two.

By 1952, the planes were increasing in size, faster, and carrying more and more passengers. The Civil Air Administration mandated that stewardesses were required on all passenger aircraft for the primary purpose of safety. The ratio was one stewardess for every fifty passengers. This required more extensive training and certification, and as a result the stewardesses joined the Transport Workers Union (TWU). Another factor that put pressure on the growing airline industry was the fact that stewardesses were marrying at an alarming rate, thus creating a large turnover. This became very costly for the airlines in training replacements.

In 1964, the Transport Workers Union sued the airlines on behalf of the stewardess under the civil rights act over their discriminatory employment practices in regard to age, weight, gender, race, and marital status. Finally, in 1968, the court ruled that marriage and forced resignation at age thirty-two was discriminatory.

Consequently, the stewardesses that were forced to resign years earlier under the old policies were given the opportunity to come back to work with full back pay and seniority. Through the persistence of the stewardess union and the civil rights movement, all discriminatory policies were eliminated.

By the end of the '70s, the term *stewardess* had been replaced by the gender-neutral alternative, *flight attendant*. In 1977, the flight attendants broke away from the Transport Workers Union and formed their own union; the Association of Professional Flight Attendants (APFA).

Chapter 1

New Beginning

When I turned eighteen years old, I left home in California, at my parents' suggestion (to avoid what they thought was a bad relationship developing between my boyfriend and me), to live with my aunt and grandfather in Massachusetts. It was my first flight, and even though I was excited about my new venture, leaving the security of my home and family made me sick to my stomach. The flight was right on time, so I didn't have a chance to think about it. With Mom and Dad's reassurance, I kissed them goodbye and quickly boarded the plane before my tears were visible. I was already starting to get homesick.

The captain's voice came over the PA system to welcome us on board and asked us to pay attention to the stewardess in the aisle for some important safety information. I watched them very closely. How beautiful and professional the stewardesses looked in their uniform! I immediately felt safe and secure knowing these stewardesses would take care of me if anything happened. I couldn't help but think what a wonderful, exciting job theirs must be…never boring.

One stewardess in particular, Bonnie, was exceptionally friendly and easy to talk to, so I asked her how she liked her job, how many days she was away from home, and if she ever got homesick.

"Oh, I love flying," she replied. "I can't think of anything else I would rather do. When I first started flying, I did get a little homesick, but you get over it quickly because you stay busy and don't have time to think about it."

"How old do you have to be?" I asked.

"Nineteen. Are you thinking about becoming a stewardess?"

"I'm only eighteen, but it sounds exciting." We both smiled, and she went back to work. When we landed in Boston, I thanked Bonnie.

"Hope to see you on the line before too long." She winked.

Aunt Judy and my grandfather were there to meet me as promised, and they were a welcoming sight. They were so excited and happy to see me that I forgot about being homesick.

My aunt worked for a publishing company and got me a job right away, no doubt because she was the boss's secretary. I was glad to have the job right away to help ward off my homesickness, but it became increasingly more difficult. As the months dragged on, I became more and more homesick.

Then one day, my boss came to me and said, "What are you doing working in a boring place like this? You're young and energetic, you should be traveling and doing exciting things like being a stewardess!" I laughed and shrugged it off.

It made me think about Bonnie, the stewardess I met on the plane. No…I thought there was no way I could do something like that!

The next day, my aunt saw an advertisement in the local newspaper. She pointed out that many airlines were looking to hire stewardesses and agreed that maybe my boss was right, I should at least apply.

"What do you have to lose? If you aren't accepted, you haven't lost anything. You'll still have a job at the printing company!" she assured me. I began to think about it more seriously. Maybe they were right. Maybe this was the change I was looking for.

Within a week, I received applications from three different airlines. Two weeks later, I received my interview dates and times for Trans World Airlines (TWA), Eastern and American airlines.

In the meantime, I wrote to Mom and Dad and told them my exciting news. My dad (being a flight engineer in the Air Force and flying all over the world) thought it was a great opportunity for me. My mother, on the other hand, was appalled. She felt that proper young ladies don't become stewardesses. The term *fly girl* and airline slogans such as "Come fly with me" and "We move our tail for you" weren't exactly what she had in mind for me. Dad assured her that flying and traveling all over the world was the best education I could get.

Chapter 2

The Interview

My first interview took place in a large beautiful hotel in Downtown Boston. The lobby of the hotel was enormous. Having been sheltered all my life, I was in awe. There was a huge chandelier hanging from the ceiling in the center of the lobby. The large spiral staircase at one end of the lobby was made of dark mahogany, as was the long registration desk and beautiful elevator doors with gold trim. As I scanned the lobby, I noticed a large white sign on a wooden easel that read "Stewardess Interviews, Second Floor, Room 295."

When I reached room 295, the door was ajar. Just outside the door was a large "Welcome" sign. I started to feel a little sick to my stomach. My nerves were starting to get the best of me when my aunt's words echoed in my ears, "What have you got to lose?" She was right. I still had my job, boring as it was, and it certainly wouldn't be the end of the world if I wasn't accepted, even though deep down I wanted to be a stewardess more than anything in the world.

The room was set up like a conference room with a long rectangular table in the center. There was a desk on one side of the room and a coffee stand on the opposite side. Seated around the table were about twenty young girls, all of whom I suspected were applicants.

A woman seated at the desk motioned me over to sign in, gave me a form, and asked me to take a seat. As I glanced around the table, I knew the competition was going to be tough. I felt like I was in a modeling agency. My confidence was starting to dwindle. What did

I have to offer? What makes me think I can compete with these other applicants? What am I doing here? Before I knew it, my anxiety level was getting the best of me. We were called one at a time.

By the time my name was called, I was a complete basket case. I was directed to an adjoining room, and the door slammed shut behind me.

The interviewer was a supervisor of stewardesses for the airlines from New York City. She was in her midthirties and looked like she stepped right out of *Vogue* magazine. She began by asking questions about my family and what I had been doing since I graduated from high school; the whole time her eyes were scanning my entire body. She paid close attention to every word and gesture I made. She smiled and abruptly thanked me for coming and said if I was accepted, I would be getting a letter in the mail. That was it. After the interview, I was physically and mentally exhausted. Fortunately, I had a couple of weeks to recuperate and regain some of my confidence before the next interview.

The second interview was also in a hotel room in Boston, but this time, there were only two other applicants. I approached this interview with a little more confidence. The interviewer was absolutely gorgeous, a little younger than the last one but also impeccably dressed.

"What makes you think you would be a good stewardess?" Her first question caught me off guard. Did I think I would be a good stewardess? I never really thought about it! Immediately, my dad came to mind. I loved flying, traveling, and meeting new people. She then asked me to walk across the room, turn, and walk back slowly. Feeling a bit self-conscious, I stood up and slowly walked across the room, trying not to trip over my feet. I could feel her watching me. She asked me if I was wearing a girdle as she tapped my butt with her hand! (I weighed 110 pounds, of course I wasn't wearing a girdle). She then asked if I did my own hair and makeup.

"Thank you for coming. If you hear from us, there will be a second interview in New York. Your airfare will be paid for, and instructions will be mailed to you." Then she added, "In the meantime, you might consider getting your chipped tooth fixed!" Chipped tooth? What chipped tooth? I never knew I had a chipped tooth!

Two more weeks went by before my third and final interview. After my last interview, my self-esteem was nonexistent. I felt fat, ugly, and stupid! I didn't want to go to the final interview, but my aunt insisted. When the time came, I didn't care whether I was hired or not.

To my surprise, this interview was a lot different. It was in an office at the hangar at Boston's Logan Airport. As I walked into the office, I noticed the nameplate on the desk, "Ed Bauer." The interviewer was a man, and he was not at all what I had expected. He was studious-looking with his black horn-rimmed glasses, slightly balding, and looked to be in his forties. He had a warm smile and a calming tone to his voice, and he expressed a genuine interest in what I had to say. Immediately, I felt relaxed. He asked me why I wanted to be a stewardess. I told him about my father, the military, and his exciting life of travel, and that I wanted to experience adventure just like him. He then abruptly flipped over his nameplate.

"I want to see how observant you are," he said. "What is my name?"

"Ed Bauer!" I piped up, hoping I pronounced it correctly. Then he asked me a strange question: "What is the most you have ever weighed?"

I thought about it a minute and said, "What I weigh right now, 110 pounds."

"Do you think you can get under 110 in the next two weeks?"

"Of course, I can!" I retorted.

He smiled and said, "You're hired!"

That was it! I'm hired! It took me a few minutes to realize he was serious. I was so excited I could hardly contain myself.

"Is that okay?" he questioned my silence.

"Yes! Oh yes!"

He asked if I could be ready to report to Stewardess College in two weeks. Without hesitation, I replied, "Absolutely!"

I felt elated. It was like a dream come true. The stewardess was a very desirable occupation for young single women. Thousands applied but few were chosen to be a part of this elite group of women.

Chapter 3

Charm Farm

The Stewardess College in 1968, referred to as the Charm Farm, was similar to a small community college. The classrooms, dorms, cafeteria, and common room were all in the same building complex. The only difference being the rules: they were strict and without exception.

Curfew was 11:00 p.m. weekdays and 1:00 a.m. on weekends. If you were leaving the campus, it was mandatory to sign out and back in when you returned. Violators were terminated. No questions asked. Security was tight. An eight-foot electric fence surrounded the school grounds, and a guard was posted at the gate. The dress code of business attire was strictly adhered to right down to the required girdle, nylons, and heels. Fingernail polish was mandatory, while earrings were not permitted.

The next six weeks of training were intensive, leaving little time for sleep. The first couple of weeks were devoted entirely to emergency procedures.

Inside a huge hangar were eight simulators (airplane mock-ups) representing the eight different aircrafts used by the airline. They served as classrooms for training purposes.

The use of emergency equipment and their location on all eight types of aircraft, how to evacuate passengers safely in ninety seconds or less, water ditching, and raft survival were all part of the curriculum.

Medical training was the next important part of our curriculum. We were given an extensive course in first aid, operating medical equipment, and training in the recognition and care of a variety of medical conditions and life-saving techniques.

The last couple of weeks were devoted to serving procedures, dealing tactfully with difficult passengers and the required paperwork. With the exception of test finals, the last week was by far the most fun, with classes on public speaking, hairstyling, and makeup.

During that time (as a marketing tool), the airline felt it was important for stewardesses to keep up with the latest fads and fashion trends of the "sexy" '60s, including minidresses, hot pants, and go-go boots. Prominent fashion designers were hired to design our uniforms, which changed every couple of years to go along with the styles. There were beauty consultants to help us look our very best. We even practiced walking down the spiral staircase with a book on our head, trying not to bounce so as not to drop the book while maintaining perfect posture.

When I was hired in the late '60s, hairstyles included the pixie and the beehive cuts (just as the name applies, hair piled high on top of your head). The beehive was a very popular updo but difficult to achieve. Hairpieces and "falls" were imperative in order to achieve the beehive look.

The beauty consultants had the final word on our individual look. Fortunately for me, it was decided that a pixie cut would suit me best. My girlfriend, on the other hand, was not as lucky. She had to achieve the beehive. It took many hours of practice, but with the help of a knee sock for lift and a "fall" to cover it, she finally acquired the look to the satisfaction of the consultant. There was, however, a price to pay. On her observation flight (a required training flight prior to graduation), she offered to hold a baby while the mother used the lavatory. The baby was infatuated with Beth's beehive, and when she gave the baby back to her mother, the baby's fingers became entangled in Beth's hair, and off flew the fall. To Beth's horror and everyone's dismay, a knotted green knee sock was exposed on the top of her head for all to see.

My problem was with the false eyelashes that were the fad at the time and required by the grooming instructors. I spent hours one night trying to get the eyelashes glued on straight. After the third set of eyelashes, I finally got it right. Knowing I wouldn't have time to get them straight before our grooming check in the morning, I decided to leave them on all night.

Five girls shared our dorm room. With only two shower stalls and four sinks, we were forced to stagger our wake-up times. Being an early riser, I volunteered to be the first up in the morning. When my alarm went off, I opened my eyes, and there on my pillow was a huge black spider. I let out a bloodcurdling scream! The lights came on, and everyone jumped out of bed. When I realized it was my left eyelash that was stuck to the pillow, I started to laugh but quickly stifled it when I saw that my roommates were not amused.

Unbelievably, smoking was permitted in the classrooms back then. Even the instructors smoked. That, too, was a fad at the time. But once in uniform, smoking was strictly prohibited in public places.

A number of students were having difficulty adhering to the almost impossible weight restrictions. Once a week, we had a grooming review that included a weight check. If your weight was borderline, you would be randomly checked two or three times during the week. If you couldn't maintain the required weight limit, you were terminated without exception!

With each passing day, attending classes became more and more anxiety-inducing; we became increasingly concerned that there would be another empty seat in the classroom, meaning another student was sent home. They either couldn't adhere to the strict curfews, were unable to maintain 90 percent pass rate, couldn't maintain weight standards, or somehow managed to displease our instructors. Without warning, they were gone, baggage and all. It kept all of us on our toes, wondering who would be next.

Finally, graduation day arrived. We were full of emotions: excitement, relief, exhaustion, anticipation, and pride all rolled up in one. We spent three hours getting ready in full dress uniform. Hair, nails, makeup, uniform, and shoes all had to be perfect to pass the final most scrutinized grooming check.

After a number of speeches and our pinning ceremony (receiving our wings), we lined up along the stairway for the traditional class picture. Following a small reception was the much-anticipated announcement, our assigned domicile. When my name was called, I was relieved to hear Boston was my new domicile assignment. It was close to home and suited me just fine. We said our tearful goodbyes and went immediately to our rooms to gather our belongings for the flight to our new home base.

Chapter 4

Life in the Fast Lane

Shortly after arriving in Boston, I found an apartment. Two senior stewardesses were looking for a third roommate to share the bills for an expensive apartment in the quaint coastal town of Marblehead, Massachusetts, on the outskirts of Boston.

It was a perfect stewardess pad—a cute little two-bedroom apartment, fifteen minutes from Logan Airport, five minutes from the beach, and right next door to a local hangout called Mattie's. My roommates, Jean and Lynn, had been flying for five years, gold wingers as they were affectionately called.

As a result of the "must be single" requirement, no children, and maximum age limit of thirty-two, the turnover rate for stewardesses was about two years. With a seniority of five years, the gold wingers had been around the block, knew the ropes, partied often, and, as I soon learned, knew how to handle the lifestyle.

My first work flight was a disaster. The plane was a BAC-111 with two stewardesses, two pilots, and sixty-nine passengers. Jane was the number one stewardess and a gold winger. I was a nervous wreck! Jane was kind and patient with me. She thought it would be better (since it was my first flight) that I should set up the breakfast trays and she would run them out. This was before mobile carts were used in-flight. Every tray had to be hand-delivered.

Knowing we had to serve sixty-nine passengers' breakfast and beverages in thirty minutes, I worked as fast as I could, trying not to spill anything. It was turbulent, making the setup slow and awkward. All of a sudden, I felt nauseous; I motioned to Jane and ran to the lavatory just in time. I quickly recovered and went back to the galley to continue setting up. The relief was temporary…again, I felt nauseous and ran back to the lavatory. My nerves were getting the best of me. Meanwhile, Jane was hustling to set up and run the trays.

As we finished serving the last row of trays, the seat belt sign came on. Our thirty-minute flight was quickly coming to an end. Up until this point, Jane had been very patient, but now that we were running out of time, she started firing orders at me.

"I'll pick up the trays! You stuff them!" She meant to put the trays back into the carts they came from. "We have to get all the trays picked up and the galley locked up before we land!"

Jane started picking up the passenger trays and stacking them on the galley floor and ran back for more. I couldn't put them away as fast as she was picking them up, and the stack started to fall.

"Don't worry about being neat, just shove them in the carts! We are running out of time!" she shouted as she ran back for more trays.

I was sitting on the floor with food all over my uniform and trays strewn all over the galley floor. I could feel us descending and knew we would be on the ground momentarily. I started to panic. Jane decided to quit picking up the trays and made an announcement to the passengers. "We'll be on the ground shortly, please fasten your seat belts and put up your tray tables. If you still have a tray, please slide it under the seat in front of you until we land."

In the meantime, I jammed the rest of the trays into the cart, secured the galley, and barely made it to my jumpseat before we landed.

This was only the first of four flights that day. I apologized to Jane for being sick and slow. I promised I would try harder on the next leg of our trip.

I began to wonder where the glamour was in this stressful job. What had I gotten myself into? Jane apologized for yelling at me, but I understood why she was upset. I was afraid I wasn't cut out for the job. She told me it was first-flight jitters and that I would be fine. She ended up being right; I calmed down and managed to get through the rest of the day without further incident.

Being a junior stewardess meant that I flew the most undesirable trips, which were the four-day puddle jumpers (short multiple flights each day) on the BAC 111, the smallest plane in the fleet. It was like running a marathon. After one of these four-day trips, my feet were killing me, and I was exhausted. I had a difficult time carrying my bags up the two flights of stairs to the apartment. It was one o'clock in the morning, and I could hear loud music and laughing coming from within. Oh god! Another party! I tried to sneak up to my room without anyone noticing.

"Gloria!" I heard Jean yell. "Where are you going? Come have a drink and meet my friends." I knew she wouldn't take no for an answer, so after a glass of wine, I managed to slip away to the quiet, safe haven of my room and locked the door behind me to prevent any unwanted guests. I think I was asleep before my head hit the pillow.

The next morning, I had to pry my bedroom door open. There were bodies lying everywhere; no doubt all of them were hung over. The apartment looked like a tornado blew through it. Bottles and cans were strewn all over the floor. The end tables were covered with overflowing ashtrays, and the smell of stale cigarette smoke filled the air. Leftover food was still sitting on the kitchen counters, and the sink was full of dishes. As I made my way through the comatose bodies, I saw Jean rushing out the door.

"Hey, where are you going?" I shouted.

"Don't worry, I have a turnaround. I'll be back tonight to clean up!"

"What about all these people?" I yelled back.

"Just let them sleep it off, they'll be gone by noon."

Having the next couple of days off, I decided to drive home to New Hampshire and visit my parents, hoping that when I returned, the apartment would be back to normal (at least until the next party).

When Jean wasn't flying, she was on the beach soaking up the sun or down at Mattie's for happy hour. I was flying back to back trips with multi-legs each day and early sign-ins. So when I wasn't flying, I was sleeping!

After a year of this chaotic lifestyle, I was anxious to get a place of my own.

Chapter 5

Probation

The first six months was my probationary period. I was on reserve (on call) twenty days out of every month and very closely monitored by my supervisor. During the probation period, we were given numerous check rides. These were flights that our supervisors were on specifically to ensure we were doing procedures by the book. Stopwatches were used to ensure our service was provided in a prompt and timely manner. A debrief followed the flight when our supervisor had the opportunity to check our required equipment, to see that our manuals were up to date, to check our grooming and critique our performance. The object was to get a perfect check ride, which I found impossible with my supervisor, Joni.

Joni was a perfectionist, very strict, and allowed no room for error. A perfect ride from her was impossible. My goal was to avoid unnecessary contact with her by staying out of trouble. At times, this was difficult. She made it a point to be at the desk every time I signed in for my flight. She wanted to make sure I was on time, had all my required equipment, had fingernail polish on (two coats), wore the required girdle, and removed my pierced earrings prior to every flight.

I should have recognized the bad omens when this particular day started. I was running late and anticipated seeing Joni. I grabbed my service apron from the dryer, rolled it up, threw it in my suitcase, and headed to the airport. As I approached the sign-in desk, I saw

Joni checking her watch. I managed to sign in with one minute to spare. She was not pleased.

After the flight took off, as I was the newbie, my coworkers decided that I would be running all the trays and they would take care of the beverages. I wasn't sure why they chose me to run the trays, but being junior, I wasn't about to argue. Halfway through the service, a little old lady tugged at my skirt.

"Excuse me, miss, but do you know you have a pair of lingerie hanging from the back of your apron?" Mortified, I reached back, grabbed the pair of pink bikini underwear (stuck by static electricity from my dryer), and immediately stuffed them in my pocket. Embarrassed, I spun around and headed for the galley. My coworkers were chuckling; it was then that I realized the reason I was chosen to run the trays.

On my next trip, I was assigned position number 2. Besides serving, I was responsible for counting, inventorying, and securing liquor money collected during the flight. We were issued padlocks to lock the money in metal boxes attached to the overhead bin while in flight. When the flight was over, it was my responsibility to take the money and deposit it in a safe in the airport operations area.

I had the padlock but forgot my combination, so I was forced to contact Joni. After a brief lecture on responsibility, she retrieved my combination numbers, and I was on my way. The next day, I received a message that Joni wanted to see me. I knew it couldn't be good news. As luck would have it, I forgot the money in the lock box on the plane. When the deposit didn't show up in the safe, they traced it back to me. Eventually, they were able to locate the aircraft and retrieve the money. This warranted a C-314 (a written letter of reprimand in my file).

Punctuality and sick time were very important issues with the airline. Even though we were flying in close proximity to thousands of passengers with a variety of health issues on a daily basis, we were unceremoniously reprimanded for calling in sick. We were allowed no more than three sick calls per year. In my first year, I caught the flu, contracted strep throat, and got tonsillitis, all of which required me to meet with Joni to discuss my declining health. She was sure my tonsils were the culprit and recommended I have my tonsils out, or I would be terminated because reoccurring sick calls would not be tolerated. A month later, I had my tonsils out. The only good thing coming out of the fact that I had surgery was that I met a wonderful man whom I married six months later and moved to New Hampshire.

My new uniform in 1977

Commuting to Boston wasn't bad nine months out of the year, but winter was another story. My first winter in New Hampshire was an exceptionally tough one. The snow levels reached an all-time high. There was so much snow that the snowplows were having trouble pushing it all back, and the snowbanks were six feet high.

On this particular morning, I left my house around 4:00 a.m. to make my flight out of Boston, ninety-seven miles away. It was still dark, and there were patches of black ice due to the warm temperatures the day before. I was only half a mile from home when my car started to fishtail. The next thing I knew, my car was buried nose first right up to the windshield in a snowbank. I couldn't believe I wasn't hurt (thanks to my seat belt!). Fortunately for me, a tractor-trailer truck came by, and the driver stopped to help. We couldn't get the door open, so he helped me out the window. He drove me to a local phone booth where I called my husband. He waited with me until my husband arrived.

I never knew who that good Samaritan was. Thanks to him, I was home safe and sound.

Even though I was bruised and shaken from the accident, I wasn't considered incapacitated, so I had to remain available for work. The next day, the airlines called me for a flight, but by then, I was too sore and stiff to work, so reluctantly I called in sick. An hour later, Joni called me. She informed me Crew Schedule told her that I had refused to take a trip, so once again, I was being served a C-314.

Being on probation finally took its toll on me. My file was getting thicker, and Joni was getting on my nerves. I was so worried about making a mistake, being late, or getting sick that I no longer enjoyed my job. At the end of my first year, I decided to turn in my resignation. Coincidentally, Joni decided to give up supervising and go back to being a stewardess around the same time.

It was Rosy, my new supervisor, who received my resignation. Rosy was laid-back, personable, and didn't care about "the book," and most importantly, she treated me with respect. She cared more about my interaction with the passengers than whether or not I was following procedures. It was her who convinced me to withdraw my resignation.

Chapter 6

Domestic Flying

Flying was so much fun! We stayed at four- and five-star hotels pre-reserved and paid for by the airline, as was our transportation to and from the airport. We were treated like royalty. Once at the hotel, as long as we left a contact number, we were free to do whatever we wanted. We enjoyed going out to dinner, taking sightseeing tours, or just walking around the various cities. Most of the time, our layovers cost more than our expense allotment for the month, but we justified it by saying it was a once-in-a-lifetime adventure. We were so young and naïve back then. We felt invincible.

One Sunday afternoon, during my first Detroit layover, I asked the concierge at the hotel where the nearest drugstore was so I could replace my torn nylons.

"Go out the lobby entrance and take a right, go about three or four blocks, take a left, and you'll see the drugstore on the corner," he explained.

It was a beautiful sunny day. As I walked block after block, I realized there were no cars and no people around. Of course, it was Sunday and this was Downtown Detroit, so all businesses were closed. It was eerie to see this big metropolitan city look like a ghost town. It was so quiet I could hear my shoes clicking on the cement walk. It seemed like I was walking forever. Did I pass the street the concierge mentioned? I was beginning to feel disoriented. Just as I was about to turn around and go back, I saw the drugstore two blocks up on the corner, just like the concierge said it was. As I approached the intersection and waited for the light to change, I noticed four young men standing around, talking and laughing right at the entrance to the drugstore. I felt a little uneasy knowing I had to pass between them to get to the store. The light changed, and I proceeded with caution. I excused myself as I cut through the men and into the store. I could feel them staring at me. Their mumbling turned to laughter as I approached the door. Needless to say, I was somewhat relieved once inside.

I purchased the nylons and continued to browse around, hoping the guys would take a hike. But no such luck…it was getting late, and I had to head back. I waited inside for the light to turn green and bolted through the door, between the men, and across the street.

My relief was short-lived when I realized I was being followed. I stepped up the pace, hoping they would fall back, but instead they stepped up their pace. I could hear them talking. I nonchalantly looked back over my shoulder. Two men were about ten feet behind me. My heart began to pound. Where did the other two men go? Were they going around to cut me off, trap me maybe? The streets were deserted. I couldn't see the hotel and I started to panic. *Oh my god*, I thought. *I'm lost!* I couldn't remember whether I should turn right or left. At the next corner, I looked up over the top of the buildings and I could see the hotel in the distance. It looked miles away, and I began to run. All of a sudden, I felt a hand on my shoulder. The voice in my head was screaming so loudly I was sure they could hear it.

"Excuse me, miss. Excuse me?"

"What!" My nerves reflected in the sound of my voice.

"We don't live around here, and I was just wondering if you knew of a restaurant nearby."

"No! I don't live…" I caught myself. I shouldn't tell them I don't live here.

"Oh, are you staying at a hotel in town?"

"Ye—I mean no," I stammered.

To my relief, I reached the hotel lobby and headed for the elevator. I pushed the button and waited. They were still behind me!

"How would you like to go to dinner with us tonight?" They were waiting with me for the elevator. I couldn't believe it! I didn't want them in the elevator with me and follow me to my room! *How am I going to get rid of them?*

Just then, the elevator doors opened, and there stood a pilot with his suitcase. What a welcome sight he was! I stepped in the elevator and gave him the biggest adrenalin hug I could muster as the doors closed behind me.

"I'm so sorry, but those guys followed me for four blocks. I couldn't get away from them. When I saw you, I knew they wouldn't follow me into the elevator. Thank you for being here!" I blurted out without taking a breath. I was still shaking.

"Glad I could help. Would you like me to walk you to your room?"

"No thanks, I'll be fine now."

That was an eye-opener for me. From then on, I was more cautious and aware of my surroundings. Every now and then, something unexpected happens again to remind me, like the time I was in New York City. Our flight was canceled due to an approaching snowstorm. Visibility deteriorated rapidly, forcing the airport to close. All the major hotels in New York were full due to flight cancelations, but the airline managed to secure a few rooms for us in a small fleabag motel near LaGuardia Airport.

The next morning, I got up early, dressed, and headed down to the lobby for a cup of coffee. I stepped into the creaking old elevator and pressed "LL" for the lobby, but the LL stood for the lower level and underground parking. When the elevator doors opened, there stood a big scruffy-looking, unshaven man wearing dirty shabby clothes. I thought he might have been a street person. He smelled of alcohol.

"Whoops, sorry, wrong floor," I said nervously as I reached for the first-floor button. Just as the doors started to close, he stepped forward and held his arms out to prevent the doors from closing. He stood there just staring at me. Immediately, I felt uneasy. My mind began to race. Was he going to get in the elevator and push the emergency stop, or was he going to pull me out of the elevator in the dark, deserted underground garage? Maybe I was blowing this out of proportion, but at any rate, I wasn't about to stand around and see.

"Well, are you in or out!" I demanded.

"Well, maybe I should join you."

"Oh, I don't think so!" I decided to take the upper hand. I ordered him to step back out of the way. After a slight hesitation, to my surprise, he obeyed. As the doors shut, I could feel myself trembling. That was a close call!

Chapter 7

Good for a Laugh

Being a flight engineer in the military, my dad loved to talk about his flying experiences with me. He had a great sense of humor, and I loved his flying stories. I was extremely naive when I first started flying, so he taught me a lot.

One day, I asked him what they do on their long flights when the tank for the toilet gets full. He told me they have a button in the cockpit that opens a small door in the lavatory tank, and when they get to a certain altitude, they dump it. I was appalled to think they dumped waste in flight.

"Won't it get on everything below?"

He laughed and said it evaporates before it hits the ground! I was still appalled.

Shortly after that conversation, I was working a flight. After we took off, a passenger got my attention and pointed outside to blue fluid blowing past the windows. I immediately went up to the cockpit to inform them they dumped the lavatory too soon. In unison, they turned and looked at me in disbelief. At that moment, I realized that my dad's sense of humor was at my expense!

When I was a junior, I flew a lot of BAC-111 trips. As I mentioned earlier, the BAC was a small British two-engine jet built strictly for short haul flights that carried sixty-nine passengers, two stewardesses, and two pilots. Our trips were four days long, making a total of twenty-one landings, which is the reason they were called puddle jumpers. By the end of the four days, the crews got to know each other pretty well. I flew a lot with Marcy on those four-day trips. She was new like me, so we got along really well.

On one such trip, we were on a layover in Syracuse, New York. Marcy and I were exhausted but hungry. The pilots offered to take us to dinner at a nice club they frequented on this layover. Although tired, on our salary, we couldn't pass up a free meal. We walked three blocks to the club. The pilots led the way to a table up front close to what looked like a stage. Wow, a dinner show! At nineteen years old, I was impressed!

After dinner, the lights went down and music started. Moments later, out came an exotic dancer. Needless to say, I was beyond stunned. Marcy and I looked at each other in shock.

Embarrassed, I looked down, staring at my plate until the music stopped. I stood up and told the pilots I was leaving; Marcy stood up, too, and followed me out the door. Reluctantly, the pilots followed. The captain apologized for not letting us know what kind of club it was and walked us back to the hotel. The captain walked Marcy to her room, and the copilot walked me to mine. I opened the door to my room, and he followed me in, laughing at my innocence. He pushed me on the bed and lay on top of me. "Get out!" I screamed. I guess I surprised him because he jumped up and promptly left my room. The next morning, he pretended nothing happened, so I ignored the incident, too, and I never flew with him again.

Chapter 8

Growing Industry

By the late '70s, the airline industry had changed dramatically. Women were taking a more influential role in society, and the stewardesses played a major part in that role. With pressure from the stewardesses' union, the courts ruled that the no marriage and no pregnancy rule and weight restrictions were all discriminatory policies. At the same time, the thirty-two-year-old maximum age was lifted, and the first female black stewardess was hired. Men were joining our ranks, thus prompting the gender-neutral name change from stewardess to flight attendant.

Also, in the '70s, the designated smoking sections were restricted to the back of the airplane and eventually led to all nonsmoking flights. It was nice not to see a cloud of smoke fill the airplane immediately after takeoff. I can't believe I spent years on a smoke-filled plane flight after flight.

Flight reservations and information became computerized, and the first wide-body jumbo jets, or luxury liners as they were referred to, changed the passengers' perception of flying.

With the introduction of the wide-body (dual aisle) airplanes and the increase in passenger capacity, the flight attendant's job changed dramatically. Beverage and dinner carts were designed to assist the flight attendant in a more efficient and elegant in-flight service.

As deregulation took hold, the airlines were looking for ways to compete for the traveling customer to gain the majority of the revenue. They began to cater to the first-class business travelers, where most of the revenue was generated.

On our long-haul flights, the Boeing 747 proved to be a selling point. The spiral staircase that led to the upper deck lounge was where first-class customers conducted much of their business. A dumb waiter was installed to help flight attendants stock the upper deck lounge and bar.

The DC-10 was another favorite with first-class swivel seats, which enabled passengers to sit at a round table and face each other while they dined. In both of these wide-body planes, three-tiered carts were used in the aisle to present a multicourse dining experience starting with champagne and caviar. The salad greens were served with a fresh Maine lobster tail and complemented with expensive wines. There was a choice of four entrées—chicken, seafood selection, pasta selection, or prime rib carved to your satisfaction—followed by a fresh fruit and cheese cart with an assortment of fine cheeses from all over the world and, of course, a select port wine. Ending this gourmet dinner was the sundae cart complete with hot fudge, butterscotch, or strawberry toppings, and, of course, whipped cream and nuts. The first-class service was comparable to a five-star restaurant.

The prime rib was one of the most popular entrée choices we offered. Everyone wanted the prime rib, but we were given only two roasts for twenty-four people, which meant some passengers were not going to get their choice. When passengers pay a lot of money to fly first class and do not get their choice of entrée, it is a major disaster.

On this particular flight, my coworker Nancy and I were working opposite aisles, serving the prime rib on three-tiered carts. We prepared our three-tiered carts with warm serving plates, horseradish sauce, au jus, and, of course, the prime rib. I stuck the serving fork into the roast and pulled the cart up to the front row to begin the service. As I bent over to pick up the first passenger's appetizer plate, my apron pocket caught the handle of the fork and flipped my prime rib onto the floor.

The passengers gasped at the sight. Nancy and I looked at each other in shock! I grabbed the roast by the fork and told the passengers I would be right back with another roast. Nancy followed me back to the galley.

"What are we going to do? We don't have another roast!"

"Well then, we have to improvise! I brewed a pot of boiling water and poured it all over the roast. "There! Just like new. You do what you have to do under the circumstances." Nancy rolled her eyes, and we went back to work.

Working first class can sometimes be trying. Some passengers are never satisfied. I heard that on another flight, during the toss salad service, a flight attendant must have reached her threshold of sanity trying to please. She took the salad tongs and started flinging the salad onto a passenger, yelling, "Take *this* and *this* and *this*!"

(Of course, she was put on an immediate leave of absence and then probably fired.)

As purser, doing my pre-flight checks list

Preparing for our elaborate First-Class Service on the Boeing 777

Chapter 9

Luxury Liners

The 747 was immense. In the back of this enormous airplane was a piano bar lounge. It was a wide-open area with lounging sofas and not a piano but a Wurlitzer organ. The passengers could get together, relax, and, if they were so inclined, could entertain the others by playing the organ.

The 747 carried close to five hundred passengers with sixteen flight attendants and four cockpit crewmembers. There were elevators in both cabins that reached the lower-lobe galleys where the meals were prepared. There were six ovens in each galley and storage for all the carts, food, and supplies for the flight. As a safety precaution, there was a trapdoor in the floor of the aisle so that the flight attendant could egress the galley in the event the elevators malfunctioned.

Each wide-bodied aircraft had a lead flight attendant referred to as the First Flight Attendant. In addition, there was an FSD or Flight Service Director. The First Flight Attendant was the service coordinator for the sixteen flight attendants. She was responsible for seeing to it that the meal service went smoothly as well as making all the onboard announcements, taking care of any problems that developed, handling the money from in-flight sales, and completing the flight report. For the convenience of so many passengers, the FSD was on board to handle inflight ticketing, reservations, and rebooking.

After eighteen years of flying, I decided to apply for the First Flight Attendant or purser (as it was later called) position. It required a recommendation from my supervisor, an interview with a panel of representatives from management, as well as the flight service department, all of which lasted eight hours. Once I qualified, I received an increase in pay for the added responsibility. Sometimes, however, the promotion wasn't worth the extra pay.

Prior to my 747 flight from Los Angeles to Boston, I was told by a supervisor that the first-class elevator on our aircraft was inoperative for our flight.

As purser, it was my duty to give a preflight briefing and inform the other flight attendants of the inoperative elevator and an alternative service plan. I mentioned that under no circumstance was anyone allowed to use the first-class galley. I informed them that due to the inoperative first-class elevator, all the first-class food and supplies were catered in the aft galley, along with the coach food and supplies. It was an extreme inconvenience but nothing we couldn't handle. Moans and groans came from the flight attendants as they anticipated the extra work involved.

Shortly after takeoff, I was shocked to learn from the FSD that a passenger had fallen through the hatch in the aisle floor above the first-class galley. It took a minute to sink in.

"What! How could that be!" The FSD explained that one of the flight attendants, thinking she could solve the elevator problem, crawled down the elevator shaft into the galley during the boarding process. When she realized it was beyond her expertise, she called another flight attendant to go to the escape hatch and guard the area so she could come back up through the hatch into the cabin aisle. While trying to make her way to the hatch, the other flight attendant encountered a woman struggling with her luggage and stopped to help. Meanwhile, the galley flight attendant opened the trapdoor, and a passenger stepped through the opening. To make matters worse, the passenger had just been released from the hospital after undergoing knee surgery! This was one flight that didn't pay to be the purser.

Chapter 10

Flying Is Not for Everyone

Not everyone loved flying as much as I did. Not all my flights ran smoothly either. On a flight to Chicago, I thought I was going to have to use my medical training. In the middle of our meal service, I was getting a tray from the galley when a young girl came rushing up to me; her eyes were wide open as if in shock with her hands around her throat. She appeared to be in great distress. Since it was during the meal service, I thought she might be choking on her food. As I stepped closer to her, preparing to give her the Heimlich maneuver, she coughed and puked chunks all over the front of my serving garment. This was the first day of a three-day trip and with only one serving garment with me. I spent my layover washing it out in the tub and blowing it dry with the hotel hairdryer.

On a DC-10 trip to Los Angeles, I happened to be flying with two flight attendants whom I have flown with many times. Chuck and Thomas were best friends and buddy bid to fly together all the time; in fact, I think Chuck talked Thomas into becoming a flight attendant.

Thomas, in his previous career, worked with his father who was a mortician. He had stories I couldn't believe, like the time he and his father were called by the police to a home where an elderly lady had passed away in bed. She was upstairs, and the heat from the summer sun had turned her body to mush. Thomas proceeded to pick her up to put her in a body bag when his father yelled out, "Don't touch…"

but before he could finish his sentence, Thomas's hand went right through her body, spewing fluids everywhere, and the stench was unbearable. It was then he decided that he was not cut out to be a mortician.

The DC-10 had a lower lobe galley where all the food was prepared and sent up to the main level in an elevator. Thomas worked the lower lobe galley position, preparing food for our service. This particular flight was extremely turbulent. I gathered from talking to Thomas on the interphone that he was a nervous flyer, especially when it was turbulent.

The captain made a "fasten seat belt" PA, saying we were just going through a patch of rough air and wanted everyone seated, including the flight attendants. I called Thomas on the interphone and told him to take the jumpseat in the galley until it passed.

The flight attendants immediately checked seat belts to make sure everyone was strapped in and no one was in the lavatories, while I checked the service center for any loose items that could become flying missiles, and then we took our seats.

When the turbulence had somewhat subsided, Chuck and I went back to the service center to call and check on Thomas. We were still holding on to the handholds when a bolt of lightning (like a ball of fire) shot through the center. It entered through the left side door of the service center and exited through the right side, making a loud *boom!* We were shocked and stunned. It was so quick we were not sure what happened. Chuck and I looked at each other. The hair on our arms was singed. The captain called back to see if everyone was all right. We were a little shook up but fine. Then I thought of Thomas down below in the galley. I immediately called him, and when there was no answer, I went down in the elevator to check on him. Poor thing was petrified. He was white as a sheet, still strapped to his jumpseat but otherwise okay.

Chuck and Thomas were on another flight with me to Dallas. Just prior to landing, we heard three dings. As a flight attendant, we know that three dings from the cockpit can't be good news. Thomas immediately perked up and wanted to know what was happening, I could hear the panic in his voice. He swore and started babbling on about flying. Chuck tried to calm him down by making light of the situation.

The captain wanted me to come up to the cockpit. *Oh geez, please don't let this be too serious*, I thought. He informed me they had a warning indicator that the nose gear was not down and locked. They were going to do a flyby so the tower could take a look. He wanted me to pass it on to the other flight attendants and make preparations for an emergency landing should it be necessary.

I explained the situation to the other flight attendants in the galley and told them to lock up and get their equipment ready just in case. Needless to say, Thomas was beside himself. I looked him in the eye, and with a calm, stern voice, I said, "Get it together! These passengers depend on us for their safety. Now get out there and do your job!"

After briefing the passengers and preparing the cabin for an emergency landing, the captain came back on the PA and said that the landing gear was in fact down but that he was not sure if it was locked, so he would give the brace command just before touchdown. I could see Thomas on his jumpseat, clearly frightened and trembling. The landing was smooth as glass and all was well. The passengers were clapping and cheering. Thomas stared at me, shaking his head.

During another flight, I happened to be in the lavatory when the plane started to make these funny little maneuvers, side to side and up and down, almost like a boat in the ocean. I went up to the cockpit to find out what was going on and realized immediately that something was wrong.

The captain took the controls while the copilot was flipping through the flight manual. I stood there in silence, waiting for them to tell me what was happening. The copilot noticed me standing there while the captain was firing questions at him, so he said, "We are going down…," and turned to answer the captain. I knew that they didn't have time to explain things to me just then, so I took it upon myself to inform the other flight attendants to be prepared for what might be an emergency landing. Of course, once again, I was flying with Chuck and Thomas. They were sitting on the front double jumpseat eating dinner. All of a sudden, Thomas jumped up from the jumpseat, threw his tray on the counter, and took off to the back of the plane. Chuck stood up and put his tray on the counter.

"I'll go back and talk to him and let the other flight attendants know," said Chuck apologetically. I remember thinking Thomas was not cut out to be a flight attendant.

We cleaned up, secured the galleys, and took our jumpseats. *Ding-ding.* After a few minutes, the call came. I grabbed the phone.

"What's up? What's wrong? What did the captain say?" It was Thomas!

"He hasn't called yet, Thomas, I'll let you know." Another couple of minutes went by. *Ding-ding.* Thomas again said, "Heard anything?"

"No, Thomas, I haven't! Don't call me again! I'll call you!" He was ticking me off. The waiting was nerve-racking; they should have called me by now. I decided to go up to the cockpit; maybe they had a few minutes to let me know what was happening and how much time we had to prepare our passengers. When I opened the cockpit door and peered in, they were laughing and joking with each other as if nothing happened.

"So I assume the crisis is over?" I said curtly.

"What crisis? There was no crisis," the captain commented. He turned and continued his conversation with the copilot. I was furious and I shouted at them. "The next time you say we are going down, you better damn well mean it!" I spun around and slammed the cockpit door behind me. A minute or so went by. *Ding-ding.* This time, it was the captain, and he explained that it had something to do with the autopilot but nothing they couldn't fix. He apologized for scaring us.

A month later, I was greeting passengers during boarding when one of the coach flight attendants told me that we were missing a flight attendant. I used the phone on the jet bridge to call operations and let them know we were missing a flight attendant. Just as I hung up, I saw Thomas coming down the jet bridge.

"Hi, Thomas, glad to see you. I thought we were going to be short a flight attendant." Without saying a word, Thomas abruptly stopped, turned around, and went back into the terminal. A few minutes later, a supervisor from Flight Service came down the jet bridge to inform us we were going to be short a flight attendant for our trip.

"What happened to Thomas? I saw him. Isn't he coming with us?"

"No, he isn't. Just know that you will be short a flight attendant."

Three months later, I ran into Chuck and asked him where Thomas was. He said every time Thomas flew with me, we had an incident, and when he saw me on the jet bridge that day, he turned around, went into the office, and turned in his resignation! Apparently, he thought I was a jinx.

Chapter 11

The Worst Air Disaster

On May 25, 1979, our nation witnessed its worst air disaster in the US history. A DC-10 jumbo jetliner, Flight 191 bound for Los Angeles, crashed on takeoff at Chicago O'Hare Airport. All 270 passengers, four cockpit crew members, and ten flight attendants were killed.

When a tragic accident occurs, we are all reminded of how precious life is and how it can be snuffed out in a split second. It's difficult for fellow crew members to carry on when such a tragedy strikes our ranks. It was especially difficult for us based in Los Angeles. Eight of the flight attendants on Flight 191 were based in San Diego, and the others, including the cockpit crew, were based in Los Angeles. They were not only coworkers but friends.

We were on the ground in San Diego, preparing to depart for Los Angeles, when we got word of the crash. We were devastated. A flight service supervisor came on board to ask how we were doing and if we were able to continue our flight to Los Angeles under the circumstances. We were all based in Los Angeles and just wanted to get home, so we agreed.

When we landed, the terminal was in utter chaos. Airline personnel were rushing around gathering the relatives and friends waiting in the lounge area for the arrival of their loved ones on Flight 191. They were totally unaware of what had just happened. The airline personnel escorted them to a secluded room where crisis management people and grief counselors were waiting to assist any way they could.

As myself and the other flight attendants were deplaning, a flight service supervisor came up to us and asked if any of us would be willing to help out by listening and consoling the relatives. My heart broke for them; I was on the verge of tears myself and I wasn't even related to them. I declined, knowing I would start crying and it would only make matters worse.

This accident caused the temporary grounding of all DC-10s until NTSB could find the exact cause of the crash. The DC-10s were grounded for one month to give airline maintenance time to check all DC-10s and make the necessary repairs.

Even though the inspections were completed and the grounding was over, many flight attendants still refused to get back on the DC-10. I, on the other hand, felt more secure than ever, knowing everything was checked and replaced or repaired.

We were one of the first crews to get back on the DC-10. Shortly after landing, we taxied to the terminal. I was helping an elderly woman walk down the jet bridge into the terminal when I heard someone say, "Oh my god! Look at that!"

I turned around to see what the passengers were looking at through the large picture window of the terminal. I couldn't believe my eyes! We were staring at a bare engine on the left side of the plane we just came in on.

I went back on the plane to ask the cockpit about it. The captain said the cowling (engine cover) fell off when we touched down. In fact, the crew was unaware of what had happened until the air traffic control tower told them that a large piece of metal just fell off engine number 1 and was lying on the runway.

It was determined that when the plane was in for the engine check, the screws that held the cowling over the engine were not tightened properly. How that cowling remained intact during our flight was beyond me. I do believe a guardian angel was with us. I was beginning to think it was sabotage, but in fact, it was an oversight. I would like to think the mechanic was fired!

Chapter 12

Hijacking

For the first time in airline history, in the early '70s, world discontent was beginning to show its ugly head. Airline safety was being threatened through a rash of hijackings. Until that time, flying was relatively safe and, other than a few medical problems, uneventful.

The hijackings were committed by people seeking asylum to a neutral country or making a statement. Typically, the hijacker was dropped off in the country of their choice. The end result was very costly for the airlines and troublesome for the passengers and crew, but seldom was anyone hurt, at least in the beginning.

During the height of the hijackings, I was working a flight from Miami to Boston. About midway through the cabin while serving beverages, I asked a passenger what he wanted to drink. He said, "I want to go to Cuba!" He had a thick South American accent, so I wasn't sure I heard him right. "Excuse me?" I prompted him to repeat what he said. He just stared at me.

In light of the recent hijackings, my training immediately kicked in. Thinking that this could be a potential hijacking, I looked around and under his seat for a suitcase, bag, or backpack, anything that could be hiding a bomb or weapon. There was a small black bag like an old-fashioned doctor's bag lying under the seat in front of him. When I asked him if the bag was his, he immediately grabbed it and wrapped his arms around the bag without saying a word. It was then I realized we could have a serious situation on our hands.

I immediately went to the cockpit to let the captain know what I had suspected. The captain asked me exactly what the passenger said to me. When I told him the passenger said he wanted to go to Cuba, the captain said, "Are you sure that is what he said and not that he wanted a Cuba libre (a Cuban drink)?" I thought about it and repeated what I had heard. He then asked me if the passenger had any bags with him. I told him the man had a small black bag that he appeared to be very protective of. It was then that he decided to make an unscheduled landing at the nearest airport to have the threat removed from the airplane. When we landed and arrived at the gate, the FBI, local police, and airport security all converged on the airplane at once, and the man was whisked away without further incident. Myself and the other flight attendants were interrogated by the FBI about the incident in addition to writing a detailed report. Five hours later, after the airplane and all baggage was searched, we were on our way.

I wonder to this day whether I thwarted a hijacking or was it just a miscommunication. The hijackings were becoming more frequent and more dangerous. In light of the rash of hijackings, the FAA incorporated additional security procedures in our annual EPTs (Emergency Procedure Training).

Chapter 13

Aggressive Behavior

Alcohol was complimentary on all flights back then, contributing to an increase in aggressive behavior. One drink on the ground is equivalent to two drinks in flight. Too much alcohol mixed with the high altitude affects people differently. Some can become lethargic, some romantic, others obnoxious, and some even violent. It's difficult to determine when a person has had enough to drink. A lot depends on his/her size, weight, and genetic makeup. We had to be vigilant when monitoring alcohol consumption in flight. The FAA would fine us if we served alcohol to an inebriated passenger. This sensitive issue had to be handled tactfully, or it could escalate into something much more serious.

In one such situation, we were boarding a flight at Dulles International Airport in Washington, DC. Our all-nighter was coast to coast with a stop in Dallas. The boarding process at Dulles is unique in that the passengers board mobile lounges at the terminal and are driven out to our remotely parked aircraft. These mobile lounges drove like buses, but once they arrived at the aircraft, the bus would elevate to reach the aircraft door. The boarding process is a busy time for flight attendants with emergency checks, predeparture beverages, hanging coats, assisting with luggage, all the while trying to screen passengers.

Shortly after takeoff, a woman brought it to our attention that the man in 28F was intoxicated and bothering the other passengers. She had noticed his behavior on the mobile lounge as well.

Since I was working first class, I checked the manifest for the name of the passenger sitting in 28F and went to talk to Mr. Davis. He was standing on his seat, bending over the seat back of a young girl who was asleep in the seat in front of him. He was in fact intoxicated and annoying. I asked him to please keep his voice down, as people were trying to sleep, and to take his seat and fasten his seat belt. To my surprise, he complied. I mentioned Mr. Davis to the captain and told him we would not be serving alcohol to Mr. Davis on our flight. He agreed.

When our beverage service began, Sophia, one of the coach flight attendants, came to me and said, "I'm not going to tell Mr. Davis that he can't have a drink. We'll have a fight on our hands!" I assured her that it would be okay, just let him know what beverages he can have. As the coach flight attendants progressed through the cabin doing the beverage service, they noticed a commotion going on and figured it had to do with Mr. Davis. Sophia again came up front and said that Mr. Davis was causing a commotion, and the beverage cart was nearing his row. I could tell she was nervous, so I told her to take my place in first class and I would take her place on the beverage cart.

I know how to handle this jerk! I thought to myself.

As the cart approached Mr. Davis's row, I told Carmen, who was working the other side of the beverage cart with me, to pull the cart past Mr. Davis's row and I would backtrack with the beverages and handle Mr. Davis. She gladly complied.

Needless to say, Mr. Davis was not a happy camper when I refused to serve him alcohol, and he again became loud and belligerent. A male passenger asked him to relax and calm down, which further aggravated him, and he began using profanity. The situation was quickly escalating. I immediately intervened and explained to Mr. Davis that if he continued with his unacceptable behavior, the captain would notify the authorities and he would be arrested when we landed in Dallas. This seemed to calm him down but only temporarily. Within minutes, he was again shouting and carrying on. He was furious that we would not serve him, so he said he was getting off the plane in Dallas so he could get a drink.

I knew from the passenger manifest that Mr. Davis was continuing on to Los Angeles with us, and I certainly didn't want a repetition of this flight. I was determined to have him removed from the aircraft permanently in Dallas.

The captain was hesitant to make the call to have Mr. Davis removed from the aircraft. He said that if Mr. Davis was that drunk, he would most likely fall asleep on the way to Los Angeles. I wasn't taking any chances; obviously the captain did not fully understand the seriousness of the situation. I decided to take the matter into my own hands. I told the captain he would have to choose between Mr. Davis and me. If Mr. Davis was allowed to continue to Los Angeles, I was going to walk off the plane in Dallas. He knew full well that I was part of the required minimum crew, so the flight would have to cancel in Dallas if I didn't go. The captain told the agent in Dallas that Mr. Davis would have to be removed from the aircraft.

Not all alcohol-related incidences were threatening in nature. An elderly gentlemen, Mr. Cornwall, in his mid-eighties, had a few drinks and was flirting with us in a harmless manner. He declined dinner and told us his beloved wife of fifty years died about ten years ago and he was meeting his new girlfriend in Boston for dinner.

Later in the flight, I noticed a long line of passengers waiting to use the lavatory.

I discovered that our elderly Romeo had been in the lavatory for about twenty minutes. Concerned for his well-being, I gently knocked on the door and asked Mr. Cornwall if he was all right. When I didn't get a response, I slowly turned the knob to the lavatory door.

Mr. Cornwall had passed out and was leaning against the door. When I opened it, he fell backward into my arms with his pants down around his ankles. He slowly opened his eyes and smiled as I laid him gently down on the floor. With the help of another flight attendant, we pulled his pants back up. Still not quite coherent, we decided to give him some oxygen. Within minutes, he was back to his old self, and I accompanied him back to his seat. When he asked for another drink, I told him I couldn't serve him any more alcohol because I didn't want him to make a bad first impression with his new girlfriend. He smiled and promptly fell asleep.

Chapter 14

Moving to California

For twenty years, I flew strictly domestic routes mostly out of Boston. In 1979, my husband and I decided to move to California with our daughter to be closer to my family and warmer weather. To my surprise, my transfer request to Los Angeles went through immediately. With such short notice, we weren't able to sell our house in New Hampshire right away, so my husband stayed behind until the house sold. We missed him terribly; I bid Boston layovers so we could be together until he could join us in California. It was a year before the house sold and he could join us.

As purser, I started flying routes to Toronto and Montreal. My favorite layover was the beautiful city of Montreal. It was a thirty-two-hour layover. There was plenty of time for sightseeing, shopping, and going out to dinner. The five-star hotel was gorgeous. As flight attendants, we were given complimentary passes to an exclusive and very popular disco club in the penthouse of the hotel. We decided to take advantage of the free pass and attend the nightclub.

On our next trip, we brought appropriate dress to go to this exclusive and trendy nightclub. We showed our pass at the door and were escorted in. We felt like VIPs. The room was very dark, and the music was deafening. In the middle of the club was a huge disco ball hanging from the ceiling, flashing color all over the room.

Once our eyes adjusted to the darkness, we could see rich black leather sofas that curved around small oval tables. In the middle of each table was a very large black glass vase with an arrangement of beautiful, fresh, exotic flowers. Windows surrounded the club, and the view of Montreal at night was breathtaking. It was a lovely evening, but I decided to call it a night early when I discovered my glass of wine was $20.

The next morning, I learned that one of our flight attendants had a little too much to drink. She left the club around 2:00 a.m. and somehow managed to find her way back to her room. While getting undressed, she had an uncontrollable desire to quench her thirst. She peeked out the door to the hallway to see how far the ice machine was and lost her balance. The door slammed shut, and there she was in the deserted hallway at two o'clock in the morning in her birthday suit!

Standing there, she began to realize the precariousness of her situation. Knowing my room was somewhere close by, she tried desperately to remember my room number. As she was knocking on the door of the room she thought was mine, a man's voice startled her. He was yelling something in French. Desperate and sobering up quickly, she went to the next door and knocked again. Just then, a hotel security guard appeared. They stood face-to-face, motionless, both in the state of shock. Suddenly, she couldn't remember her own room number. Trying desperately to stifle his amusement and keep his eyes on the carpet, the security guard used his walkie-talkie to obtain her room number. Within minutes, she was back in her room.

Our VIP pass to the Regine's disco club on our Montreal layover

My next trip to Montreal, however, was an emotionally distressing one. The entire crew had decided to go out to dinner together. It was still daylight on our way back and a beautiful warm summer night. I heard a plane overhead and instinctively looked up. Out of the corner of my eye, I caught a glimpse of a man falling through the air as if in slow motion and landing abruptly on the stone wall surrounding the hotel. I couldn't believe my eyes. My brain was trying to comprehend what my eyes just witnessed.

As we approached the hotel, I could see the man was lying on his back in a pool of blood, his legs dangling over the edge of the wall. I felt sick to my stomach. I thought I was going to lose my dinner. People began gathering all around and whispering to each other. One man from the crowd knelt down beside him and shook his head. At that moment, the police and the ambulance arrived, began dispersing the crowd. We heard later that the man had jumped from his hotel window.

That night, I couldn't sleep at all. I was trembling uncontrollably and scared to death being alone. How could life be so bad that someone would want to end it like that? It was weeks before I could sleep through the night. It was a horrific sight that I will never forget.

Chapter 15

International Flying

After a couple of years in California, my husband and I decided that the fast pace, the high cost of living, and the freeway traffic just weren't conducive to our lifestyle, so we moved back to New Hampshire, and once again I was flying out of Boston.

Shortly after my transfer back to Boston, I was looking for more adventure and excitement that domestic flying was no longer providing me. A friend of mine convinced me to transfer to the International Operation of our airline and fly to destinations in Europe and Asia. It sounded like a good idea. I flew back to the Charm Farm in Dallas for more training and got my International qualification. It was fun, interesting, and just what I was looking for.

We were trained on all overwater-equipped aircraft, including water ditching and life raft survival. The survival techniques were accomplished in huge pool inside the hangar on a full-size life raft. We had to jump in the water and climb into the life raft by using the lifelines attached to the sides of the raft. The raft tubes were four feet above the water, so we had to climb up a rope ladder to get over them into the raft. Definitely not as easy as one might think. With a lot of teamwork, we were able to get everyone into the raft. Once in the raft, we had to erect the canopy and locate and use all the equipment provided in a compartment inside the raft, including applying a patch to one of the tubes and collecting rainwater for drinking. It was a lot of fun and prepared us well for what might happen should we be forced to land in the water.

Culture classes were also a major part of our training. If we were going to fly to different countries with different cultures, we should at least learn the dos and don'ts; after all, we were foreigners in their country. It was such a great learning experience.

I was looking forward to new and exciting destinations, not to mention an increase in pay. I started by flying to the Caribbean in the winter months and Europe in the summer. It was the best of both worlds.

Getting ready for take-off

The Caribbean was a welcome change from the cold winter months in New England. I enjoyed our layovers immensely: parasailing in Aruba, snorkeling in St. Thomas, and sunbathing in San Juan and Barbados.

Packing only our bathing suits, sandals, and sunglasses, we left Boston in temperatures below zero and landed in the tropics. We landed early in the afternoon changed into our bathing suits and headed for the beach. We sat on lounge chairs with a margarita in one hand and a camera in the other while watching another gorgeous sunset. That was the life! This was the part of flying that was so much fun.

The next day in Aruba, one of our passengers boarded the flight in a wheelchair. She was red as a beet, and her skin was flaking off. When we inquired about her condition, she said that she was wind-surfing, got tired, lay down on her board, and fell asleep. When she woke up, she had drifted out to sea and couldn't get back to shore. Her husband notified the surfboard company that his wife hadn't returned, so they went out looking for her. Her body was literally fried.

From Boston, we also had the opportunity to fly to South and Central America to cities like Guatemala, Costa Rica, Puerto Plata, Jamaica, and Santo Domingo in the Dominican Republic. It definitely was a cultural experience, as many of these countries were third world countries. Their houses were made mostly of bamboo with openings for windows, no doors, and no indoor plumbing. Tugging at my heartstrings were the little barefoot children that surrounded us, begging for pennies. They were so excited to see the "rich Americans." They offered little homemade gifts in exchange for a few American cents. It is truly amazing how much we take for granted.

On one of our layovers in Puerto Plata, my flying partner Lynda, and I decided to rent scooters, ride to town, and experience a little local culture. After paying our rental fees, we headed off on what we had hoped would be an unforgettable adventure. The rental clerk told us that town was only a few miles away and suggested we stick to the main road.

It didn't take long for us to realize that the only driving rule was to stay on the right side of the road. There were no speed limits and no stoplights or signs. No right of way, just first come first served. All the vehicles were old, and many looked like they had been in demolition derbies with no brake lights. Traffic was heavy and the pace was fast. It was organized chaos. The roads were primitive, mostly rocks and dirt. Our New England chuckholes didn't even compare to the huge ruts and gullies created by the heavy rains in the area. All in all, it made for a very stressful journey.

We managed to dodge the cars while avoiding most of the ruts, but the pace was too much for us, and by the time we reached town, our enthusiasm for sightseeing disappeared. We were already anticipating our return, trying to decide whether it would be safer to ride or walk our scooters back to the hotel. It was getting late, and we couldn't help but think if the taillights didn't work then it probably would be safe to assume the same of the headlights. Ultimately, we decided in order to get back to the hotel before sunset, it would be quicker if we rode the scooters. It was an exhausting adventure.

Enjoying our beautiful Puerta Plata layover.

On our flight home, I was approached by an American passenger. He curled up his index finger and motioned me to follow him back to the lavatory. He pointed and asked me to look in. A bit hesitant, I slowly opened the door and was shocked at what I saw. I couldn't believe my eyes. The toilet was totally full to the rim with human waste. Every cubbyhole and crevice in the lavatory was stuffed with used toilet paper. I was mortified!

The toilets on the A-300 have an enormous suction capability, so for fear of rupturing the waste tank, I chose not to flush the toilet but instead closed the door and locked off the lavatory to prevent further use.

"Aren't you going to clean it up?" asked the passenger.

"Would you?"

"No, but that is not my job!" he replied.

"Well, it's not my job either!"

The more seasoned flight attendants informed me that many of these passengers didn't know what a flushing toilet was and that constant monitoring of the lavatories prevent such things from happening. To top it off, whoever designed the Airbus lavatories put the flushing instructions plaque on the wall behind the seat so when the toilet seat was up, the instructions were covered.

A few weeks later, on another Airbus flight from Boston, we were headed for St. Thomas with a stop in New York. About fifteen minutes after takeoff from Boston, the other flight attendants and myself got up from our jumpseats and headed to the back galley to prepare for our beverage service. Suddenly, the plane started to jerk to the right, then left and right again, whipping us from one side of the plane to the other. I remember being thrown off my feet and seeing my coworkers fly past me.

Just as suddenly as it started, the plane stopped jerking. Unaware of what had just happened, I grabbed onto a seatback and pulled myself up. I could see that a couple of my coworkers were hurt. Although shaken up, I was doing okay. While the flight attendants were helping one another, I walked through the cabin to make sure our passengers were all okay. Fortunately, it happened right after takeoff, so the passengers were still buckled, in and everyone was fine. The captain called back to check on us, and I gave him a report on the injured flight attendants. Micki hit her head pretty hard on the metal handhold in the galley, so her head was bleeding significantly. We found out later that she also had broken bones in her right hand. Another flight attendant sprained her ankle and couldn't walk. The rest of us were banged and bruised, but thankfully no one was critically injured. The captain decided to return to Boston so we could get medical assistance.

Later we learned that while the plane was on autopilot, there was a malfunction in the yaw damper software that caused the back of the plane to jerk back and forth. Once the autopilot was released, everything returned to normal.

There was an FAA inquiry, and the problem was immediately corrected.

I spent a lot of time flying to the Caribbean on this A300 Airbus

Chapter 16

Europe

Going to Europe put a whole new spin on flying for me. It was unlike any other destination I had been to so far. At first, I just flew to London and Paris. Both were beautiful cities, and the sightseeing was fantastic. We managed to pick up a few foreign words here and there, just enough to get by. Getting around on the Tube (London subway) and the Metro (Paris subway) was a feat in itself. Learning the different currencies and trying to get used to the time change were all part of the adventure.

On a layover in Paris, we decided to take a train to do some sightseeing. After flying all night and arriving late morning in Paris, the usual scenario was to go right to bed and nap for a few hours and then go out in the city. But by the time we got up from our nap, it was getting dark and there was not enough time to sightsee. So on this particular trip, we decided to forgo the nap and stay up. We immediately changed our clothes, bought train tickets, and were on our way. We were so tired that we dozed off, and to our surprise, we were awakened by the conductor at the end of the line in the country. It was getting dark, so again no time to sightsee. We managed to catch the last train back to the city. Another lesson learned!

The next trip, we took a short nap before venturing out. We walked along the Champs-Élysées and went up the Eiffel Tower. We visited the Musée d'Orsay, the Louvre, and the Arc De Triomphe and still had time for dinner at one of the many lovely sidewalk cafes.

Dining in Paris was an expensive but wonderful experience. It was considered an event taking anywhere from two to four hours. We decided to splurge one night and went to a quaint little bistro in the middle of the city recommended to us by one of our passengers. The waiters wore white shirts and bowties with a tray in one hand and a white linen cloth draped over the other. Dinner was, of course, served with wine. Each course, although small compared to American standards, was elegantly prepared. For the final course, a large serving platter was brought to the table with a selection of tasty French pastries. Needless to say, the event was well worth the money.

It is not uncommon in Paris to see patrons come into fine restaurants with their well-dressed pooches, who lay quietly at their feet while their owners dine, sometimes even sitting at the table in an outdoor café.

London was as much fun as Paris but a little more laid-back. We took a cruise on the Thames, saw Trafalgar Square, Big Ben, Buckingham Palace, and Hyde Park. But the highlight of our day was, while we were walking in Kensington Park, Princess Di drove by and waved at us.

Shopping at the famous Harrods department store was an experience in itself. It was a window-shopper's delight—too expensive to buy but well worth the look. It was seven magnificent floors with a multitude of rooms, each with a different décor. It's a great place to find a gift for the person who has everything.

On the streets of London are these interesting-looking tall oval cylinders, which I later discovered were public toilets. For twenty pence (roughly thirty cents), the door automatically opens, and once inside, the door closes and the patron has approximately five minutes to complete their business before the automatic disinfecting shower sprays the entire inside of the stall. They are antiseptically cleaned and also prevent long waiting lines.

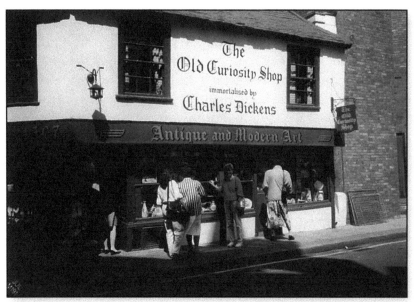

Shopping at the famous Dickens Curiosity Shop on our London Layover

*One of our many sight-seeing tours in London included
the Parliament Building across the Thames*

View from our hotel room in Rome after our CRAF Mission for Desert Storm

*Visiting the beautiful Sistine Chapel in
Vatican City on a Layover in Rome*

Chapter 17

Chicago

These travels only whet my appetite for new destinations. In 1995, I transferred to Chicago, which opened up a whole new phase of flying for me. My transfer to Chicago required me to commute from my home in New Hampshire to Boston where I would then board my commuter flight to Chicago. It was eight hours before my workday began. People thought I was crazy to put up with the commute. At first, I thought so too. But the variety of trips out of Chicago made the commute bearable. Not only did I fly to England and France, but I also had the opportunity to fly to Scotland, Sweden, Belgium, Switzerland, Italy, Germany, India, China, and Japan.

Unlike foreign carriers where their trips were seven to ten days in duration, the majority of our international trips were three and four days. We flew round trip to one overseas destination at a time with a twenty-four- or thirty-six-hour layover.

Once I got used to the commute, it became second nature. The airfare was free because I had over thirty years of seniority with the company, so the cost was not a factor.

Tardiness, however, was another story. It has never been tolerated in the airline business for obvious reason. Even though I was a commuter, it was my responsibility alone to make my trips on time. The weatherman became my best friend and the computer my right hand. But every now and then, bad weather inevitably caused a problem with my commute.

One of my most memorable commutes was in January. As usual, I arrived in Boston in plenty of time to catch my commuter flight to Chicago. The airplane was late arriving at the gate because the ground crew were clearing snow from the ramp. As a result, boarding was delayed. It was a small plane, and the flight was full, so the agent had to check my suitcase. Once on board, I took my assigned seat like the rest of the passengers and buckled in. After another short delay, the door was closed, and the captain made an announcement that we were waiting to be deiced. Forty minutes later, we were taxiing out for takeoff. We hadn't gone very far when the captain once again came over the PA.

"Ladies and gentlemen, due to weather conditions in Chicago, air traffic control has informed us that they are temporarily halting all westbound departures. As soon as we are given an update, we'll pass it on. In the meantime, you are welcome to use your cell phones if you wish to make a call."

Moans and groans could be heard throughout the plane. This was one of those few times I wished I wasn't in my uniform. It seems to invite conversation whether you want it or not. The lady sitting next to me was becoming agitated and inquired about the captain's PA.

"Can they do that?" she asked.

"Do what?"

"Make us wait here until they decide to let us go?"

With patience, I replied, "Yes, they can. It's safer waiting here on the ground than in the air over Chicago, don't you think?"

"Well, how long will we be here? I have a connection to St. Louis!"

"Yes, ma'am, I have a connection to Tokyo," I retorted.

"What happens if you don't make it?"

I'll be in more trouble than you!" I answered her with a smile.

I used my cell phone to call the international SOD (supervisor on duty) and let her know I was sitting on the plane in Boston waiting for our flight to depart. I informed her that I was scheduled to fly the purser position to Tokyo at 11:45 a.m. She said she would keep an eye on my flight in case they needed to replace me. I wasn't too concerned at that point; I still had some time to play with. I had just dozed off when the captain made a PA that we would be taking off momentarily. "Well, it's about time," I heard the lady stammer. I just smiled and fell back to sleep.

"Ladies and gentlemen, we are about fifty miles east of O'Hare and have been in a holding pattern for the last twenty-five minutes. We are getting low on fuel, so we will be flying on to Madison where we will refuel and then head back to O'Hare. We apologize for the delay. We should be on the ground in Madison in approximately ten minutes. Thank you for your patience." This did not go well with my seat partner.

"Oh, this is just great! What next?!" retorted the lady. I ignored her comment and looked at my watch. Now I was getting a bit anxious about making my trip. My only hope was that the weather in Chicago was also delaying outbound flights, including my flight to Tokyo. Again I called the SOD to see if my Tokyo flight had a departure delay. She told me that the Tokyo flight would be departing on time. She explained that there were no reserve flight attendants to take my place, so the flight would be going out short one flight attendant if I didn't make it on time. The added pressure didn't help.

Once on the ground in Madison, the captain made another announcement informing us that we were number 25 in line for refueling. At this point, not only the lady next to me but the entire planeload of passengers were ready to jump ship.

I had to do something. I left my seat to talk with the agent about my dilemma.

"Is there a plane all fueled and ready to depart to Chicago?" I inquired.

"As a matter of fact, there is a flight that is all fueled up and just requested to taxi out for Chicago right there." The agent pointed to a Super 80 parked right next to us.

"Oh *please*, can you get me on that flight so I can make my trip to Tokyo?" I pleaded with the agent.

"Come with me." The agent called our captain and asked permission to lower the back airstairs so I could deplane, which he did. I ran down the stairs while the agent used her walkie-talkie to call the captain of the Super 80 to allow me to board his flight to Chicago. Within minutes, I was on my way to Chicago. Miraculously, I made my flight to Tokyo. My suitcase, however, was still in the belly of the plane on the ground in Madison. Although inconvenience, not all was lost. Through prior experience, I learned to put the bare essentials in my carry-on tote.

Our return trip was late getting into Chicago, so I missed my commuter flight to Boston. Again, the weather was beginning to cause departure delays, and flights were already starting to cancel. After my twelve-hour flight from Tokyo, I had to wait all day in Chicago for my commuter flight. I finally managed to get the last flight to Boston. It was a Fokker 100, which is a small jet, and the only seat left was a jumpseat, which I shared with a working flight attendant. I was so tired that midway through the flight I fell asleep and fell off the jumpseat and onto the floor. I made such a thud that it attracted the attention of the entire coach cabin. Definitely one of my most embarrassing moments!

Flying to Tokyo was fascinating. I convinced my best friend and fellow flight attendant, Lynda, to come with me on one of my trips with our two daughters so they, too, could experience the Japanese culture.

We took the complimentary bus ride to the small town of Narita (outskirts of Tokyo) and did a walking tour of one of the many beautiful temples and the sacred grounds. We stopped at a restaurant and treated our girls to a traditional kneel-down Japanese dinner. Outside the restaurant, the chefs were preparing the delicacy of the day, eel. There was a huge barrel of seawater full of eels. The chef reached in and pulled out a live eel. He speared it to the table and began to filet it in front of us. Although gross, Lynda and I found eel to be quite tasty. Our daughters, however, decided that was one entrée they were not interested in trying.

There were very few Western-style (American) toilets in the little town of Narita. Rather than explain it to the girls, we decided to let them experience it for themselves. My daughter went into the bathroom and moments later came out with a puzzled look on her face.

"What's with the bathroom? No toilets!" Jenn said.

Innocently, I asked, "What do you mean?"

"The toilet seat is on the floor covering a hole in the ground!"

We had to laugh and explain to her that the culture is to squat over the seat, not sit on it like we do in America.

"I'll get my pants wet! I'm not using that!" she announced.

"Well, it's either that or wait till we get back to the hotel."

She decided she couldn't wait. And of course, we looked at her pants when she came out. Thankfully, she reemerged unscathed.

We all had a wonderful time, but it was a long way to go for a twelve-hour sightseeing tour.

Chapter 18

Escapades in Europe

In this business, there is never a dull moment. On a flight to Rome, I was working first class and we were taxiing out. I had just completed my safety checks and was taking my jumpseat when all of a sudden, a large heavyset woman came running past me into the lavatory and slammed the door.

"Excuse me, ma'am! You'll have to return to your seat, we are getting ready to take off." There was no response. I rapped on the door. "Excuse me, ma'am, is everything okay?" Again, no response. "I must ask you to take your seat at once. It's an FAA regulation that all passengers must be seated with their seat belt fastened for takeoff, with no exceptions." I pleaded with her. Immediately, I called the cockpit to let the captain know we had a passenger in the lavatory.

"Well, tell her to sit down! We are getting ready to take off!" he shouted.

"I did but she doesn't respond. I think she might be sick."

"Well, if she is sick, then we will need to go back to the gate. It's your call."

I knew if we had to go back to the gate, it would be at least an hour delay at the gate, then we would have to get back in line again for takeoff. Again, I knocked on the door and told the woman we would be taking her back to the gate. Suddenly, the lavatory door opened, and the woman came out and took her seat. She admitted that she and her husband had just spent a week in Mexico and she came down with Montezuma's revenge. The doctor had prescribed Imodium, but it hadn't kicked in yet. I called the captain back and told him we were all set to go.

As I headed back to my jumpseat, I reached over to shut the lavatory door and I couldn't believe my eyes. Indeed, Mrs. Allan's Imodium had not taken effect. Not one area inside the lavatory had been spared, not the floor, not the walls, and not even the ceiling. It was as if she had exploded. I locked off the lavatory and took my seat, contemplating our seven-hour flight with a full load and only one usable lavatory.

While in Rome, we spent most of the afternoon at Vatican City and even caught a glimpse of Pope John Paul waving from his window in the Basilica. We ended the day at a nice Italian restaurant. Unfortunately, none of us spoke Italian, only a few words here and there, just enough to get by. We managed to place our order by pointing at the items on the menu. Jeanette wanted a little more detail. She pointed to four or five items on the menu, trying to get the waiter to describe an entrée. The waiter only nodded his head. In frustration, we convinced her to just pick something, and if she didn't like it, we were willing to share.

After a couple of glasses of wine, our meals finally arrived. The waiter served all but Jeanette's entrée. A few minutes later, he came back carrying a huge tray and, to our surprise, placed five entrees in front of Jeanette. It was then we realized a lack of communication could be a real problem. The waiter had assumed she wanted everything she pointed to on the menu. Sheepishly, Jeanette picked the one she wanted and convinced the waiter to take the rest back. The waiter was somewhat indignant. We left a hefty tip, hoping to smooth over the ill feelings. We didn't dare go back to that restaurant again.

The trip back to Chicago was uneventful. When we arrived, I discovered all the flights to Boston were canceled due to the weather. A huge nor'easter had hit the East Coast, and I was forced to spend the night in Chicago. I called my husband, and he informed me that Logan Airport was closed and probably would be for the next three or four days.

I decided since I couldn't get back home to Boston, I might as well pick up an available three-day trip to Stockholm. Stockholm was another beautiful city. We took a cruise on a small tour boat through the waterways surrounding the city. We were freezing, but we learned a lot of history about Sweden. Stockholm itself is made up of fifteen thousand islands connected by bridges. We went into a lock connecting the fresh waterways to the sea.

The tour guide explained that Stockholm was an important part of Viking history. They had built a warship so big and heavy that it sank ten feet from the shore. It is still there today and has since been turned into a wonderful museum.

Frankfurt, Germany, was another city full of history. On the bus ride into the city from the airport, we passed ruins from World War II still standing. There were some old motorcycles and bicycles still used today that were ridden during the war. It gave me an eerie feeling to see remnants of World War II still around. It reminded me of all those hundreds of thousands of soldiers who gave their lives in that war.

Belgium was one of many other wonderful destinations. I loved the fresh-made Belgium waffles we bought from vendors on the streets of Brussels.

Other destinations I loved—the beautiful beaches in Honolulu and Maui, Hawaii, and the cultural center in Narita, Japan, where we were dressed in the traditional wedding kimono and learned all about the fascinating Japanese culture.

Learning all the steps to putting on a Kimono at the
cultural center on our layover in Narita, Japan

Wearing the traditional Wedding Kimono

Chapter 19

Putting Out Fires

Flying wasn't always fun and games. As I previously touched on, alcohol can create a volatile situation, especially on an airplane at thirty thousand feet. On my flight to Paris, a middle-aged woman came running back to the galley to tell us that a young man was beating up his girlfriend.

When I reached the couple, the man was yelling at a girl, who was crying uncontrollably. With the help of a male flight attendant, we managed to separate them.

I moved the girl to an empty first-class seat so she could tell me what happened.

Sally reluctantly admitted that her boyfriend becomes aggressive when he drinks. I told her we would have the police meet the airplane in Paris to have him arrested. She begged me not to involve the police.

Arriving in a foreign country posed another problem. There is no FAA like we have in the United States. Once we land on foreign soil, local law enforcement take over, and they handle such situations differently. So after conferring with the captain, it was decided that if she was not willing to press charges, there was nothing more we could do except to keep them separated for the rest of the flight.

On another flight from London to Boston, I was working the purser position when I heard a commotion in the business class cabin. During the meal service, while one of the business class flight attendants was picking up the china plates and stacking them in a metal bin on top of the serving cart, a passenger started yelling at her because he said she was making too much noise. She apologized and tried to stack the china a little more carefully so as to minimize the noise. The passenger still was not satisfied with her efforts, and when she suggested she could find him another seat away from the noisy galley, he freaked out. He reached across the cart and started beating her over the head with his rolled-up newspaper, yelling obscenities. Then he proceeded to ram the cart into her, pushing her against the wall. Fortunately, there was an off-duty Boston police officer sitting across the galley who heard the commotion. He immediately grabbed the passenger's arms and wrapped them behind his back. I grabbed a pair of plastic handcuffs from our service kit, and the police officer cuffed the passenger. When things calmed down, we checked on Rachel to make sure she was okay.

When we landed in Boston, the airport police, security officers, and state police were all there waiting for us. They whisked away our irate passenger.

Not all incidents involving alcohol were as serious as that one. We were on our way back from Japan when a coach flight attendant came up to our first-class galley with a strange look on her face. When I asked her what was wrong, she wanted me to come back to the aft galley, as there was something she wanted me to see. When I reached the back, there was a Japanese man, obviously inebriated, sitting on the jumpseat with his pants down around his ankles, masturbating. Mortified, I told one of the male flight attendants to see that the situation was taken care of immediately.

The problems seemed to subside when the airline started charging for alcoholic beverages.

Chapter 20

9/11/2001

The events of 9/11 changed not only the airlines but the world, neither of which would ever be the same. On September 11, 2001, I was over the Pacific Ocean on a flight from Narita, Japan, to Chicago. We were about an hour from the west coastline of the United States when our captain got word of the horrific events that had just taken place.

I was just settling down in the bunk room on the 777 aircraft with two other flight attendants for our break when a coworker appeared in the doorway to tell us a plane had just hit one of the twin towers in New York City. Our immediate thought was that a small aircraft with an inexperienced pilot hit one of the towers. Within minutes, the same flight attendant came back to say another plane just hit the second tower and that they were in fact commercial airliners. There was complete silence while we were trying to decipher what we had just heard. This was not an accident but instead an act of terrorism against the United States.

The captain called us up to the cockpit one at a time to share with us the limited information he had obtained from air traffic control. Since the controllers weren't sure how many planes were involved in this major attack, they assumed other planes may have terrorists on board as well. It was decided that the US airspace would shut down to all inbound aircraft. In addition, all aircraft already in the US airspace were grounded immediately. This was a huge undertaking and one that air traffic control personnel were not given enough credit for accomplishing.

Not knowing if we had a terrorist on board our flight, the captain decided to make an announcement to our passengers, telling them that we had a very ill crew member on board and that we would be making an unscheduled landing in Vancouver, Canada, for medical assistance. Once on the ground, he would have more information to pass on to them.

The captain instructed us to guard our door exits, not let anyone near them once on the ground, and to be aware of any unusual or strange behavior. While sitting on my jumpseat in preparation for landing, I glanced around the cabin at each passenger, looking for anything unusual. Instead, everyone was sitting quietly, doing their own thing, completely oblivious of what had just occurred.

While keeping an eye on the cabin, I began to think about my family back home. Where were they? Had they heard about the attack? I thought about my parents in South Carolina, who I was sure were watching the news. They never really knew my flight schedule or where I was at any given time. I was sure they were worried sick.

After what seemed an eternity, we landed and taxied to a remote area of Vancouver International Airport and waited for word from the captain. As I looked out the window, I could see we weren't alone. There were twenty or maybe thirty aircraft parked every which way on the tarmac.

Just then, the captain came on the PA and told the passengers the real reason we were on the ground in Canada. The United States was under attack by terrorists.

A loud gasp of disbelief came from the cabin. Immediately, passengers were on their cell phones to find out more information. Within minutes, the passengers knew more than we did. By then, the third plane had hit the Pentagon, and the fourth plane went down in Pennsylvania. I tried to call home, but there was no answer. Immediately, I missed my family terribly and wanted to go home. In a way, I was glad there was no answer because that meant they were not home and probably hadn't heard the news.

Shortly thereafter, I learned one of the planes that went into the tower was Flight 11 out of Boston bound for Los Angeles. My heart ached. For years, I flew that popular flight before transferring to Chicago. I was sure I knew the flight attendants aboard that fatal flight.

Once on the ground in Vancouver, we had to wait our turn for a vacant gate. All the gates at Vancouver airport were occupied with aircraft grounded from all over the world. The Canadian ground personnel were working feverishly to get planes unloaded and off the gate for the next airplane. After about six hours, we taxied to the gate. The airport personnel were wonderful and very accommodating. Air Canada flights were canceled temporarily so that their gates could be used for all the grounded foreign carriers.

We spent a couple of days in Vancouver until the US airspace opened for inbound flights. We were the first flight to land at Chicago O'Hare Airport after 9/11. The terminal was deserted. There were no people or agents around. No flights departing. The TV monitors were all blank. It was an eerie feeling.

The other flight attendants and myself went down to the flight operations area. There were a couple of service managers in the office who directed us to a conference room where there were grief counselors to offer support if we needed it. I sat and listened to coworkers tell their stories of disbelief until I couldn't stand it anymore.

I went up into the terminal to use my cell phone. I talked to my husband and daughters to assure them I was fine. It helped to talk with my family, but I really wanted to go home. I thought about renting a car and driving home, but I didn't feel I could make it alone. I sat in a chair in the empty waiting lounge and started to cry. For the first time in my life, I felt helpless and afraid.

A short while later, agents began to appear, and flights started to show up on the monitor, but Logan Airport in Boston was still closed, and no one could tell me when it would reopen. On the departure monitor, I noticed a flight to Portland, Maine. If I could only get to Portland, I knew I could make it home from there. I ran to the gate and managed to get on the flight.

I met a woman on the flight who had rented a car and was headed to Boston and offered me a ride. Gladly, I accepted. She dropped me off where my car was parked. I don't remember driving home that day. I was just glad to see my family.

Later, I learned that I did in fact know four of the flight attendants on Flight 11. My heart broke for all the crew members involved and their families and the families of the passengers on all those fateful flights.

The crew members, our brave comrades, and those courageous passengers took it upon themselves to fight terrorism on board their aircraft. How could such a thing happen in our country, land of the free and home of the brave? Just unimaginable!

Chapter 21

CRAF Missions

Following the tragic events of 9/11, the tightened security measures practically crippled airline travel. With the escalating war in Iraq and Afghanistan, unrest in all parts of the world, and a growing dislike for American policy, travel abroad was becoming increasingly risky. The traveling public decided to stay closer to home and drive instead of fly on their vacations. It took a long time to get the traveling public's confidence back, and when it returned, the newly implemented security procedures were intolerable.

When war was waged against the terrorists in Iraq, thousands of US troops from all over the country were being deployed. With not enough military transport planes to handle all the tanks, Humvees, support equipment, and troops, the military contracted civilian aircraft to help transport the troops to Iraq via Kuwait. Since this was a risky operation, the airlines asked for volunteers to work these CRAF (Civil Air Reserve Fleet) missions. There was no lack of volunteers. Everyone wanted to be part of CRAF, but only the most senior pilots and flight attendants were given the honor of flying America's bravest and best men and women to Kuwait to fight for our country.

Fortunately for me, I was senior enough to work many of these patriotic flights. We were issued chemical suits and instructions on how to put them on in case there was an air raid while our plane was on the ground in Kuwait and special ID (Geneva Convention) cards in case we were captured.

For the safety of the aircraft, crew, and soldiers, the object was to get the plane on the ground, unload the troops and their gear, refuel, and take off in a minimal amount of time. The whole operation went relatively well.

On one of my CRAF missions, however, we had a scare. We were in line to land when we heard a siren go off, indicating an air raid warning of an incoming missile. In preparation for landing, the captain told us to put on our chemical suits and masks as a safety precaution. One of the flight attendants, Britta, was claustrophobic and wouldn't put on her gas mask. The missile went right over our aircraft and hit a shopping mall located on the other side of the airport. After landing and all was declared safe, we hustled to get the troops unloaded, refueled, and took off again immediately.

The captain had Britta removed from the CRAF operation. He didn't want to be responsible for someone who refused to take orders.

After the first year, we began bringing our soldiers back from the Middle East.

Even though the mood was more jubilant, you could see in their eyes that life for them had changed forever. Although this was a small contribution to the patriotic cause, it was the most rewarding experience of my life.

I am surrounded by these brave soldiers on their
way to carry out Operation Desert Storm

Getting a lesson on gun handling from a soldier on board our flight

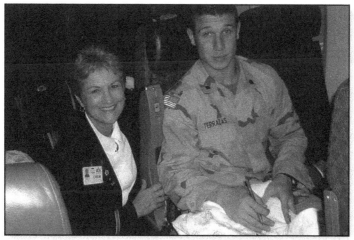

*Getting an autograph from a soldier on the way to
Kuwait for Operation Iraqi Freedom*

Chapter 22

Sky Marshals

After 9/11, our flights were a lot different. Everyone was leery about returning to flying. There were sky marshals on every flight, dressed in ordinary clothes and carried concealed weapons.

Depending on the type of aircraft, there were between two and four marshals on each flight—one in first class and one in coach. The flight attendants knew where they were sitting, but the passengers were unaware that they were even on board. Initially, it was nerve-racking, but as time went on, we began to feel a lot safer, knowing they were on board to help us.

On one of my flights from Chicago to London, I was the purser working in the galley when a passenger wearing a full-length black robe and a black headdress approached the galley. When he turned toward the door of the aircraft, I noticed he had what looked like a black wire wrapped around his finger, going up his arm under his garment and up around his head and attached to a mini black box on his forehead.

Seeing this, I started to freak out. We were all on edge, but this was about to put me over the edge. I went into the cabin to locate the marshal. I knelt down and quietly explained what I had seen. He agreed to follow me to the galley to observe the man in black. The marshal told me not to worry, everything was fine. He explained that some religious practices require Muslims to pray five times a day, and when they pray, they must face the city of Mecca, which is what this man was doing. When I inquired about the black box on his forehead, he said it was called a Kaaba, which has historical significance for Muslims. After talking with the marshal, I relaxed.

Later, when security started to loosen up, the sky marshals started to disappear from our flights. The cockpit doors were now impenetrable, and we as flight attendants were on our own in the cabin to fend for ourselves should there be a terrorist on board.

We had to continue to be extremely vigilant on every flight thereafter.

Chapter 23

Taj Mahal or Bust

In 2005, we were awarded a new route to New Delhi, India. I was excited to experience yet another new culture. I must admit it wasn't at all what I had expected. My vision of India was what you see on TV promoting tourism in this vast beautiful country.

It was midnight when we landed. The airport was in complete chaos. It was packed with people coming and going, pulling carts stacked with four and five suitcases high. We struggled to make our way outside where the smog was so thick we could barely see our bus a hundred feet away. The air was so acrid it made my eyes water and my throat burn. We learned that it was worse at night when it's cold because they would burn tires to keep warm. Can you imagine, *tires*! Wood has to be trucked into the city and, therefore, was too costly to use for heating. The toxic smoke was sickening.

After a twenty-five-minute ride, we reached the hotel. To our surprise, it was a beautiful five-star hotel right in the middle of what looked like a very poor section of town. It was a VIP hotel where many distinguished guests stay while in New Delhi. It was surrounded by hundreds of security guards. The doormen wore typical Indian uniforms that were maroon with gold trim and a gold cummerbund with a turban to match. They greeted us in Indian fashion with palms together as if in prayer and bowed their heads as they said, "Namaste," which means welcome.

While we were waiting for our hotel room keys and converting our American money into rupee, we inquired about going to see the

Taj Mahal. We were told it was a four-hour drive and they would set up a driver for us but we would have to leave by 6:00 a.m. in order to see it all and get back in time for pickup at 9:00 p.m. It was now 2:00 a.m., but we decided to go for it, anyway. I wasn't sure I would be able to get out of bed with just three hours of sleep after working all night (a fifteen-hour flight), but I knew it was a chance of a lifetime, so I would have to make the sacrifice.

When the alarm went off, I didn't know where I was. It took a few minutes to get oriented. I dragged myself out of bed, took a shower, and made my way downstairs. I took solace in the thought that I could sleep in the cab on our four-hour ride.

After negotiating a price with the driver, we were off. Due to the early hour on a Sunday morning, there was very little traffic, so the driver was cruising about sixty miles per hour on the narrow dirt road. It was scary at times, especially when we drove through densely populated towns. That didn't seem to matter, though, to the cab driver. Being the back-seat driver that I am, I wasn't able to sleep. There were no speed limit signs and no stoplights. There were camels, cows, and monkeys walking all over the road. As we got closer to the Taj Mahal, the pedestrian traffic picked up but still didn't faze the driver. When we finally arrived in Agra, we met with our tour guide, Arnav, who spoke much better English than our driver.

Modes of transportation in New Delhi

On our way to the Taj Mahal we saw Camels hard at work

Sharing the road on our frightening cab ride to Agra

The Taj Mahal was indeed spectacular, built of all white marble with inlaid gemstones. All sides of the entrance to the palace were made of marble carved in different flower designs with lattice work and inlaid colored gemstones trimmed in gold. It was built in the seventeenth century by hand with picks, hammers, chisels, and wire for cutting. The tour guide told us that at the time, the emperor, Shah Jahan, had the Taj Mahal built in memory of his beloved wife,

Mumtaz Mahal, who died in childbirth. It is said that the emperor was so devastated when his wife died that the entire country was in mourning for two years.

Beautiful inlay gemstones on the ivory marble walls of the Taj Mahal

Shah got the most skilled architects, inlay craftsmen, calligraphers, stone carvers, and masons from all parts of India and as far away as Persia and Turkey. All the marble and materials were carried in from all parts of India on the backs of one thousand elephants. It took twenty-two years to build this architectural wonder. People said that this ambitious project was that of a "crazy lover." I hoped this was not true.

Arnav told us that after the Taj was built, it was said that Shah cut off the hands of the twenty thousand workers involved in the construction so that it could not be duplicated.

The Taj itself was perfectly symmetrical as well as the surrounding buildings built of red sandstone. It was quite a feat built in 1631 without all the equipment we have today. No doubt that is why it is considered one of the New Seven Wonders of the World.

After spending two hours admiring this magnificent palace, we were forced to head back so we could get in a nap before our long flight home. The drive back was the most frightening experience of my life. The fact that I was overtired probably didn't help. The driver was going much too fast for the conditions. Not only was the traffic heavy in the towns, but there were also hundreds of pedestrians walking on both sides of the road and others running across the road right in front of us. When we got beyond the city limits, there were elephants and camels on the sides of the road carrying huge over-sized bundles. There were cows and dogs meandering aimlessly in the roads. The driver was weaving in and out around cars and at the same time dodging the animals and people that were everywhere. All the while, you could hear endless beeping horns. By the time we reached the hotel, I was physically and emotionally exhausted. It took me two days to recuperate after that trip, but I am glad we were able to see the Taj Mahal.

*Magnificent Taj Mahal. The picture doesn't
do it justice. It was breath taking.*

Epilogue

During my career, I felt like I was leading two separate lives. It wasn't always like that. When I first got married, my husband worked six days a week, twelve and fourteen hours a day, leaving little time for us. I loved traveling and didn't mind being away from home. But that all changed when my daughters were born. It was difficult leaving home for two, three, and four days at a time. In addition to flying and being a wife, now I was a mother, housekeeper, cook, and chief bottle washer. My days off were filled with doctor appointments, school functions, attending sports events, and carpooling.

Before each trip, I prepared to shift gears from my home responsibilities to my work responsibilities, making a mental note not to forget my passport, ID card, and F/A Manual, which were all mandatory. Also, I had to keep in mind the kind of aircraft I would be working on, the position, and the responsibilities for that position. I had to know the weather conditions for my commute and at my destination in order to pack the necessary clothes.

When I returned home, I shifted gears back to my home-life, sometimes forgetting where I left off. My daughter would say, "Mom, don't you remember! I told you before you left that I had this appointment!" My calendar was always full of important dates, and my refrigerator door was covered with Post-it notes.

It takes a very understanding, loving, and supportive husband to be married to a flight attendant. He has to be willing to accept change at a moment's notice. I am fortunate to be married to such a man. Dick was always able to cope and never complained.

My daughters, Maria and Jennifer, are grown-up now. There are no more tears when I leave, just a loving, "See you when you get back, Mom, and have a good trip!" instead. I was able to give my daughters a chance to see parts of the world that they may never have the opportunity to see again.

After forty-one years of traveling, I decided to hang up my wings and enjoy my retirement!

This pandemic, as awful as it is, has given me the opportunity to stay home and finish this book that has taken me years to complete. I pray for all those lives lost due to this terrible virus and that a vaccine is coming soon.

About the Author

Author and her husband left New England and moved to Montana to be with their two daughters, son-in-law, and two grandsons. Since she spent most of her life traveling, she enjoys staying close to home. When she is not spending time with her grandsons, she likes to sew and enjoys making jigsaw puzzles with her husband.